Creating

IT HAS A *magical* WAY OF FILLING YOU UP INSIDE.

After finishing an artful project where you are allowed to express yourself -- be it arranging a bouquet of homegrown flowers, putting together a beautiful card for someone special, capturing the perfect photo on film or designing a whimsical and colorful wall hanging -- you just feel different, don't you? PROUD, UNDERSTOOD, FULFILLED. You relish the feeling a while. You get used to that feeling and begin feeling the need to create with a medium…any medium. You become fulfilled in a deep and artistic way. And so your passion becomes a way of thinking and being. ¶ Ever notice how some people -- those artsy ones -- have a knack for applying their passion and creating no matter what the medium? The artists you're about to meet have a true knack for this. It's what they do. Their love of art seeps into all aspects of who they are! And they just don't seem whole unless art is front and center on their long list of daily tasks. With a premise for living like that, writing, dressing, celebrating and decorating their homes all become a way of personal, blissful expression. We thought it would only be fitting to give them some papers and embellishments and let them show us the way. ¶ Whether you share that passion, feel a need to develop your passion or just want to sit back and admire theirs, we think you'll agree with us on this one. IT'S A WAY OF LIFE. A CREATIVE LIFE. A *Foof-a-Life*. This book is your time to be inspired. Let them show you. A time to share, a time to reflect, a time to shine. *Turn the page. It's time to begin.*

one

Chapter One: 4
A Time to Share

two

Chapter two: 22
A Time to Reflect

Chapter Three: 38
A Time to Shine

three

A Time to Share

It's as much fun to *give* as it is to *receive*. Do you agree? We certainly think so! Especially when the **gifts** are as *sweet* and *sentimental* as those in this chapter.

These generous artists are in the giving mood and freely share their best ideas for meaningful gifts for any occasion. You'll find mini books, houses of love, vintage bling, party hats, cakes and more. There's no time like the present, and there's no present like time. Give a little of your time while making one of these heartfelt projects. ¶ And instead of keeping all the fun to yourself, invite a couple friends (artsy or not) and set out a basket of supplies or assemble a kit for each friend. Imagine the catching up you can do while whipping out one of these projects together. Reward the artful students afterwards with cupcakes and lemonade. These projects are fun to create and will make ideal gifts to give or receive!

Happy Birthday by Candice

supplies > Chipboard Alphabet & Paper: Foof-a-La® & Hallmark; Streamers: Party City

Make the hat shape by shaping patterned paper around a Styrofoam cone and adhere it to a sturdy base. To finish the edges of the hat, use pre-made vintage confetti or make your own with streamers and tissue paper. Give it a personal touch by adding pictures and wording with adorned glitter accents.

^ A GOOD HOME *by* MARILYN
supplies > Die-cuts, Buttons, Twill & Rub-ons: Foof-a-La®; Adhesive: E6000 & Golden; Ink: Tsukineko; Metal Corners: Provo Craft; Pens: Zig; Stamps: Hero Arts

Cut windows in a papier-mâché house or cardboard box. Cover outside of house with patterned paper and add rub-ons. Make a front door from corrugated cardboard and a button. For the roof, use a strong adhesive to adhere metal corners to sides of house. Glue button cards to metal corners as shown. Embellish rest of house as desired.

< HANGER *by* JENNIFER
supplies > Die-cut Tag, Stickers & Rub-ons: Foof-a-La®

Add rub-ons to a wooden hanger. Drill a hole through one end of the hanger to insert the wire from the berry stem and nail the other side into the hanger using a small finishing nail. Decorate a tag and hang from top. Apply large letter stickers to cardstock and trim with scalloped scissors. Finish with ribbon and mini clothes pins.

< Desk Set *by* **Jackie**

supplies > Brads: Lasting Impressions; Envelope Templates: ScrapPagerz; Paper, Tags, Stickers, Buttons & Rub-ons: Foof-a-La®

Make a set of note cards and envelopes using an envelope template. For the matching tin, adhere a strip of paper to the outside of a small tin. Punch a flower from patterned paper and add a button center. To make the notepad cover, adhere two tags together and score two folds to fit the notepad. Secure notepad to the bottom side of the cover; embellish with a tied button. Embellish paper clips by hot gluing two buttons to the end and tying with hemp cording. Dress up a clipboard with rub-ons and letter stickers. Tightly roll a rectangle of patterned paper and slip it inside a pen shaft to create a matching pen. To make the address book, cover a small composition book with patterned paper. Apply rub-ons for the title and add letter sticker dividers.

^ Childhood *by* **Candice**

supplies > Adhesive: Art Glitter Designer; Bags: Paper Reflections; Paper, Chipboard, Alphabet, Rub-ons, Twill, Buttons & Canvas Flowers: Foof-a-La®

To make cupcake toppers, use a liquid adhesive to apply glitter to chipboard accents and let dry. Attach to painted sticks. For pinwheel effect, cut a strip of paper to 1"x12". Fold paper into an accordion, making the creases crisp and the folds small. Glue the end of the accordion strip together to create a circle. Affix a chipboard circle to the back for support. Glue glittered chipboard embellishment to the front of the pinwheel. Use a strong adhesive to glue the chipboard to the stick. Use tape for extra hold. Adorn with string, ribbon or tulle. For the favor bags, apply rub-ons to store-bought paper bags.

SEEDS OF LOVE *by* MARILYN

supplies > Font: 1942 Report; Ink: Tsukineko; Paper, Stickers, Tags, Buttons, Canvas Flowers, Rub-ons & Brads: Foof-a-La®; Stamps: Purple Onion Designs and PSX

Paint and decorate an old book cover with fibers, buttons and images cut from paper. Tear out pages leaving only the amount you wish to use. Trim those pages, leaving about 1" of the page remaining in the binding. Adhere the new pages to the remaining 1" of the original book page. Make new pages with seed packets, cardstock or patterned paper. Fill pages with photos, quotes, stamped images, ephemera, fibers, canvas flower, paint and rub-ons.

Who doesn't love a good book? They inspire us. They take us to other places and times. They give us something to dream about or learn from. Marilyn's book is no exception. She shared with us this great altered book binding technique. Altered books are so open ended and have unlimited potential. Think of it as a blank book, just waiting for your story to be told and shared.

Use a small vintage book that is still in pretty good shape (binding must be intact and not falling apart.) Rip out about 2/3" of the inside text pages to make room for added bulk. Leave the end papers intact to hold the binding and inside text pages to the book covers. Tear out the remaining inside text pages one at a time, only this time don't tear out the whole page -- leave about 1" of the page remaining in the binding. These 1" page "flaps" will be where you will adhere your seed packets and other papers. This practice of adding your own pages to these page flaps is called "tipping in". Use a glue stick, Perfect Paper Adhesive, soft gel medium or any white glue to adhere the new pages to the flaps. For a different look, eyelets or brads could be used to attach the new pages.

Use patterned papers, textured papers, paper ephemera, paper doilies, tags and the seed packets as tip-in pages. Use decorative-edged scissors on some of the edges for variety. Embellish the new pages with photos, along with quotes that support your theme. Further embellish pages with tags, silk flowers, eyelets, brads, buttons, fabric flourishes, canvas flowers, rub-ons, stamped images, paint, water-soluble crayons and doodles. On the seed packets, use some of the actual decoration of the packets as part of your artwork or totally cover with paint.

Alter the color of the book cover with white paint and water-soluble crayons. To allow the textures of the original cover to show through the paint, rub some of it off shortly after applying it to the covers. Embellish cover with patterns cut from paper, rickrack, buttons and canvas flowers.

^ Jar Baby by Teresa
supplies > Adhesive: Diamond Glaze; Paper & Letters: Foof-a-La®

Silhouette a photo and add wings and a hat cut from patterned paper. Color cheeks with colored pencil. Apply Diamond Glaze to seal the image. Cut a 1/2" slit in bottom center of chipboard. Cut a 1"x 3" rectangle from chipboard and cut a slit in the rectangle. Slide photo slit into rectangle base slit so photo will stand up. Place in jar and fill with buttons to cover chipboard base. Cut a square of paper with decorative scissors and place over top of jar. Carefully screw lid to jar and tie ribbon around lid.

> Bebe by Jennifer
supplies > Cloth Tape: Paper Source; Glitter: Ranger; Paper, Die-Cut Tags & Chipboard Letters: Foof-a-La®; Ribbon: May Arts

Cover front of square hardcover journal or sketchbook with patterned paper, applying cloth book tape to the spine. Trace tag shape onto front cover, paint, then apply a thin line of glitter around the edges. Glue star brads to each end of the painted tag shape and apply chipboard letters.

For the wand, wrap a wooden dowel with patterned paper. Apply a small band of cloth book tape to each end of the dowel. Insert dowel into a star-shaped ornament; secure with hot glue. Tie ribbons to dowel below the ornament.

∧ Little Bucket of Hugs and Kisses *by* **Kim**

supplies > Adhesive: Mod Podge; Ink: Paper Salon; Paper Frills: Doodlebug Designs; Papier-Mâché Bucket: Paper Source; Paper, Stickers & Tag: Foof-a-La®; String: Raffit Ribbon

Decoupage bucket and lid with inked patterned paper. Remove handle from bucket. Cut a long piece of floral wire and fold in half. String several buttons on wire to desired handle length. Attach wire in holes from original bucket handle. Add a tag and netting to handle.

< Flowers for Thee *by* **Kim**

supplies > Adhesive: Mod Podge, Stiffy Fabric Stiffener; Ink: Ranger, Stewart Superior; Paper, Stickers, Buttons & Tags: Foof-a-La®; String: Raffit Ribbon

Rub paintbrush bristle tips in stamp ink. Add green ink to handle. Cut out five petal shapes from felt using pinking shears. Pour fabric stiffener in a plastic sandwich bag and add petals. Remove petals and squeeze excess stiffener out of petals using fingers. Attach petals to paintbrush using string or linen thread. Let dry overnight. Cut leaf from patterned paper and cut green floral wire to desired length. Apply decoupage medium to wrong sides of leaf paper. Sandwich floral wire between leaf papers and let dry. Wrap leaf around paintbrush flower stem and shape to desired form. Paint tin and let dry. Decoupage hearts and letter stickers to tin. Add tags and a string of buttons to the handle. Fill tin with netting and paintbrush flowers.

^ **BIRTHDAY CAKE** *by* **JACKIE**
supplies > Font: 2Peas Sonnets Script; Gems: Westrim; Paper & Buttons: Foof-a-La®; Pen: Zig

Cover three round, wooden boxes with coordinating patterned papers. For the crown portion, glue strips of the same paper back-to-back and freehand cut the crown points; top points with buttons or gems. Cut the scalloped edge from scalloped paper and punch a hole in each scallop; adhere to second cake layer. Adhere a length of decorative bead trim to the outer edge of the lid on the largest box. Use a selection of buttons and gems to cover the bead trim binding. Print small sentiment and cut into the shape of a small banner. Trace the edge of the banner with a thin black marker. Double fold the banner on each end of the sentiment to create a small pop-up. Adhere only the flag portions of the banner to the bottom edge of the crown.

< **GUSSIE UP PURSE** *by* **KIM**
supplies > Adhesive: Mod Podge; Ink: Paper Salon; Papier-Mâché Purse: Darice; Paper, Buttons, Rub-ons: Foof-a-La®; Stamps: Stampotique

Paint papier-mâché purse with cream paint; let dry. Roughly paint pink paint on top of cream. Decoupage patterned paper to surface. Stamp flower and text on pink cardstock, then coat with decoupage medium. Slide pink cardstock in front of purse. Thread buttons, then glue around heart cutout. Create message on inside of purse with rub-ons. Add netting, trim and butterfly to handle.

∧ **BUTTON BRACELET AND RING** *by* EMILY
supplies > Buttons: Foof-a-La®; Wire & Gem: Westrim

For the bracelet, thread lots of buttons onto 26 gauge wire. Using size 3 (or similar) knitting needles, knit 3 or 4 basic stitches to cast on. Knit as if you were making a thin scarf and on every few stitches, pull up a button. Make long enough for a bracelet, then cast off as you would do a scarf. Snip off the excess wire, leaving a few inches to weave back into the bracelet ensuring a secure closure.

To make the ring, choose a large button with an indent in the middle to make a place in which you can glue a jewel. Take several inches of wire and wrap loosely around a finger to make several loops. With the end piece of the wire, loop through the "loose wreath" to hold it in place. Thread the end into the button hole and secure. Glue jewel into place and allow to dry.

> **FLOWERS THAT NEVER FADE** *by* JENNI
supplies > Ink: Memories; Paper & Buttons: Foof-a-La®; Stamps: PSX

Cover naked chipboard flowers with patterned paper, sanding all of the edges. Embellish flower centers with buttons, vintage flower appliqués, crystals or small photos applied to chipboard circles. Add a wire stem to flower, securing the end to the back with a strong piece of tape. Adhere cardstock leaves to some flowers with names or messages.

^ Good Friends Wall Hanging *by* **Teresa**

supplies > Paper, Alphabet, Buttons & Chipboard Icons: Foof-a-La®

Remove cover from an old hardcover book. Collage and stitch patterned papers and old book pages; mount on book cover. Adhere a vintage cabinet card of two girls. Add text cut from school paper under photo. Affix square and circle chipboard shapes to top of project. Drill two holes through the book cover and string with chain to hang. Add buttons and ribbons to finish.

> Friendship Canvases *by* **Becky**

supplies > Paper, Twill, Buttons & Canvas Flowers: Foof-a-La®; Pens: Sakura

Dry brush paint randomly over 8"x10" canvases. When dry, adhere patterned paper (strips or squares) with a strong, wet adhesive. Let dry, then embellish with rub-ons, felt letters, handwritten journaling, canvas flowers, buttons and twill.

A Time to Reflect

James M. Barrie quipped, "God gave us *memory* so that we might have *roses* in December." Fortunately, we can reminisce on past experiences and remember the sweet **memories** we've made.

Aren't we lucky to essentially live life twice -- once in the moment and again as we fashion a memorable project with the photos? ¶ In this busy life of always moving forward, it's more than worthwhile to slow down and take a look at where we've been. Holidays, Grandma's flowers, photos from days gone by, birds of spring, family trees -- these are all great reasons to reflect. Think of *A Time to Reflect* as a bouquet of roses dedicated to the memories of those we love. All captured forever. Creatively. It's truly one of the best parts of life.

Chocolate Box *by* **Jackie**

supplies > Box: Debbie Mumm; Paper: Foof-a-La®

Sand and paint all edges of a round gift box and lid, then cover the inside and outside with patterned paper. Cut photos into circles and add glitter to the edges. Using 3D foam adhesive, adhere pictures into cupcake liners. Adhere cupcake liner to inside of box with double-sided tape. Tie a ribbon bow on the lid and add a glittered tag.

⌃ FAMILY TREE SHADOWBOX *by* JACKIE

supplies > Flower: Advantus; Font: 2Peas Flea Market; Paper & Twill: Foof-a-La®; Ribbon: May Arts & AC; Stickers: Foof-a-La® & AC

Cover the background of the shadowbox with strips and circles of patterned paper. Cover a chipboard monogram with paper. Paint a small tree branch/twig with green acrylic paint; hot glue into a tiny clay pot and fill with decorative moss. Hot glue the pot to the inner bottom edge of frame. Hang a framed photo, tag and paper flowers from branches. Apply stickers to bottom right corner.

⌃ SONGBIRD BANNER *by* MARILYN

supplies > Beads & Garland: Westrim; Paper & Buttons: Foof-a-La®

Cut garland to length desired. Cut each flag from patterned paper, fold over garland and glue both sides together. Cut circles from sheet music, adhere one to each flag and glue a bird in the center. Adhere beads to perimeter of each circle and tie a ribbon at the top. Stitch buttons to garland.

^ THE CREATIVITY FAIRY *by* JENNIFER

supplies > Font: Rosewood; Paper & Die-cut Wings: Foof-a-La®; Pin: MM; Vintage Image: www.designerdigitals.com

Decoupage patterned paper over glass-covered candle. Print vintage photo to size and cut out. Apply thick layer of coarse craft glitter to die-cut fairy wings. When completely dry, glue to back of photo. Using a template, trace a large oval onto coordinating patterned paper, cut out and adhere tissue paper garland around edges. Adhere fairy image to oval with dimensional glue dots and use hot glue to attach entire piece to papered candle. Create and print banner using photo-editing program, trim and apply to oval using dimensional glue dots. Apply thin lines of glitter to dress and headband of fairy image. Secure a decorative stick pin to mimic a magic wand.

> HOME SWEET HOME *by* KIM

supplies > Adhesive: Mod Podge; Clock Face: www.smallstudioproductions.com; Ink: Paper Salon, Ranger; Paper, Stickers, Die-cuts & Buttons: Foof-a-La®

Decoupage boards with patterned paper. Add embellishments and photos. Glue or tape house together after decorated.

^ **Henry is One** by **Emily**

supplies > Paint: Derivan Matisse; Paper & Die-cuts: Foof-a-La®

Cut three 5"x 7" pieces of cardstock to form the base for mini collages. Arrange patterned paper and photos to cover the cardstock. Finger paint white paint around the edges and into the cracks of the papers/photos. Immediately wipe excess paint with baby wipe, leaving a streaky, milky effect. Sand edges of chipboard pieces and add to collages. Sit collages into frame and it's ready to hang.

< **You are My Home** by **Kelli**

supplies > Ink: Memories; Paper: Foof-a-La®; Pens: AC; Photo: Tara Whitney

To make the card, trim cardstock to 12"x 8$^{1}/_{2}$". Cover inside with blue and green cardstock and patterned paper. With the fold towards you, measure 2" in from the right side. With the card folded in half, cut two slits about $^{1}/_{2}$" apart and 2" long from the fold towards the outside edges of the card. Move 1" to the left and cut two more slits exactly the same size. Cut another slit 2" in from the left side, making the cuts $^{1}/_{2}$" apart and $^{1}/_{2}$" long. Open card and push the slits inward.

Create a house and tree from patterned paper and adhere to the pop-ups. Cover outside of card with red patterned paper and add twill tape across the center to keep card closed.

TWILL POSIES & HEART PIN *by* TERESA
supplies for posies > Pin Back: Westrim; Twill: Foof-a-La® *supplies for heart pin* > Pipe Cleaner & Pin Back: Westrim; Twill: Foof-a-La®

For the Posies: Cut a small circle of fabric for background. Stitch wide, gathered twill to fabric circle in two or three layers. Embellish the posies with silver garland, rickrack, buttons, sequins, rhinestones, ball chain and leaves.

Love the idea of designing with twill? Here's another variation that's quick, easy and fun to make. Think of twill as a skinny strip of fabric. Its options for creativity are nearly endless.

For the heart shape: Teresa wanted the twill larger to cover the flower so she added strips of the twill, side by side, to adhesive-backed felt and created a classic heart and wings pin. It would be a dynamic focal point on a pillow, book cover or mixed with other embellishments on a project. Adding a pin back to the back of this piece makes it easy to wear your artful heart on a scarf, hat, lapel or sweater!

Cut adhesive-backed felt into heart shape with wings and cut wide twill into heart shape with one strip for each half of the heart. Remove sticky backing and add cut twill shapes. Repeat process for wings of heart, cutting red-cream twill into wings. Run back side of twill (with no print) over a red inkpad to change its color. With pencil, write word lightly over inked twill. Run sides of felt heart and wings over top of black inkpad to finish sides and cover up white felt. Age the heart and wings with the black ink. Stitch over the pencil marks with black embroidery floss. Stitch embroidered twill over heart. Add silver pipe cleaner around the heart, starting at the bottom point of the heart and wrapping it around the heart then twisting to secure at the bottom.

1. Cut a 2½" muslin or canvas circle. Gather twill and stitch to fabric, working around entire perimeter of fabric circle.

2. Do another circle of twill inside first circle overlapping the two layers.

3. Use strong adhesive to adhere baubles, buttons, etc. to the center of the posy.

4. Hide stitching on back with a circle of self-adhesive felt. Add pin back.

^ **BOX OF CHOCOLATES** *by* **CANDICE**
supplies > Paint: Derivan Matisse; Paper, Die-cuts: Foof-a-La®

Sand and paint all edges of a round gift box and lid, then cover the inside and outside with patterned paper. Cut photos into circles and add glitter to the edges. Using 3D foam adhesive, adhere pictures into cupcake liners. Adhere cupcake liner to inside of box with double-sided tape. Tie a ribbon bow on the lid and add a glittered tag.

< **REFLECTOR ORNAMENTS** *by* **JENNI**
supplies > Aluminum Light Reflectors: Ebay; Paper, Rub-ons, Glitter Letters & Chipboard Monograms: Foof-a-La®

Using vintage aluminum light reflectors as the base, add photos to large chipboard circles and embellish with rub-ons and glitter monograms or add a chipboard monogram to the center with a hand-cut patterned paper background. Punch a hole in tin at the top and add an ornament hook. Punch a hole in the bottom of some tins and add a chipboard circle embellished with a photo and mercury glass beads.

^ **OPA & OMA** *by* **JENNIFER**
supplies > Die-cut: CI; Paper & Twill: Foof-a-La®; Vintage Bird: Cavallini & Co.

Paint a 12" x 12" stretched canvas with a neutral color, making sure to paint each outer edge of the canvas. When dry, adhere patterned paper and book paper over canvas with decoupage medium. Apply white paint to a random section of the collage -- thin around the edges and opaque in the middle. Layer photo and paper embellishments and adhere to canvas. Use hot glue to attach the twill, sprig of pine, berries and glitter star. Journal around photo and embellishments. Spray canvas with archival spray.

< **SWEET DREAMS** *by* **KIM**
supplies > Chipboard Alphabet, Stickers & Tags: Foof-a-La®; Glitter Paper: Darice; String: Raffit Ribbon

Paint a large papier-mâché ornament. Cut circle shape from glitter sticker paper and glue to front of ornament. Affix glitter alphabet shapes on top. Make a hanger from metallic garland. Embellish with tags, buttons and butterflies.

A Time to Shine

"A Time to Shine" is all about *dazzling... you!* For this last chapter, we gave the artists an open-ended challenge. They took the challenge <u>and</u> *ran with it.*

We gave them a chance to use their favorite technique or feature a project that makes them beam with satisfaction. We are delighted to show you what they came up with: art to wear, star-shaped books, cheerful clowns, a treasure box suitcase, paper cones brimming with spring flowers, and oh, those three wooden chairs! ¶ It's impressive to see how just a few pieces of Foof-a-La® can inspire these women to create something wonderful. Pull out your paper, twill, ribbon, buttons, stickers and tags and start imagining. You're sure to find your own light bulb moment here...shine on!

Cigarette Case Collage *by* Jenni

supplies > Chipboard House: Jenni Bowlin Studio; Paper, Stickers & Monogram: Foof-a-La®; Stamps: Hero Arts

Crop a photo to fit in one side of an old cigarette case or other tin. Cut a simple house shape from chipboard and embellish with patterned paper, a monogram and journaling. Attach house to other side of tin. Wrap a vintage costume necklace around one side of tin for final embellishment.

^ Candles by Candice

supplies > Paper, Canvas Flowers, Chipboard Alphabet & Tags: Foof-a-La®; Ribbon: Midori; Roses: Paper Source

Cover candles with strips of paper and tags. Use ribbon, canvas flowers, glitter chipboard alphabet letters and other flowers to decorate the candles.

> Clown Box by Candice

supplies > Glitter, Kraft Boxes: Joanns; Honeycomb: Posi-Bendr Co.; Lace: Wyla; Paper, Rub-ons, Canvas Flowers & Tag: Foof-a-La®

Cover a gift box with strips of paper. To make the hats, cover a small styrofoam cone and adorn with vintage confetti or handmade confetti (streamers). For the clown head, spraypaint any round object (e.g. a plastic apple) with antique white. Make the collar from pink honeycomb and lace; glue to lid. Make the clown's face using fleur-de-lis rub-ons, pom-pom nose, canvas flower cheeks and glitter eyebrows and smile. Glue the clown head onto the collar, then glue the hat onto the clown head.

41

^ Wish Fairies *by* Marilyn
supplies > Adhesive: Golden; Beads: Westrim; Colorless Blender Pen: ChartPak; Font: AL Uncle Charles; Ink: Ranger; Paper & Stickers: Foof-a-La®

Cut tag shapes from old book paper. Punch hole at top and add hole reinforcer that has been inked with sepia ink. Add strip of paper at bottom of tag. Print images of children onto matte photo paper and cut out. Add to tag. Cut wings and add to each child as shown. Place a letter or number sticker on each child. Transfer word to bottom of tag using a "toner" copy of the word (word must be printed with toner printer or copier in reverse first) and a colorless blender marker. Tie length of ribbon to top of each tag though the punched hole. Tie with embellished embroidery floss. Tie tags onto branches.

> Baby Cake and Animals *by* Kelli
supplies > Adhesive: Mod Podge; Paint: Crayola and Advantus; Paper, Stickers & Buttons: Foof-a-La®

To make cake, roll diapers together to make the layers of the cake. Tape them into place with masking tape. Make three sections in successively smaller sizes. Cut scalloped paper into strips. With one part brown watercolor paint and two parts water, paint along the edges of the scalloped paper. Wrap each cake layer with the papers, securing with glue dots. Add buttons. Using a sharp paper cutter, cut strips of paper into very skinny pieces. Wrap these long strips in small bunches around a finger or pen to make them curl. Place on top of cake layers. Tape a tag to the top of a wooden skewer. Add letter stickers and buttons. Insert in top of cake.

To make the animals, cut animal shape from wood. Sand all sides and edges; add wheels. Mix one part white paint with three parts water to make a white wash. Cover the animals in several coats. Cut out same animal shape from patterned paper, but just a little smaller. Decoupage to the side of animal. Water down brown paint (one part watercolor paint to two parts water) and paint the edges of the paper. Attach buttons for the eyes.

^ TAG BOOK *by* **EMILY**
supplies > Adhesive: Matisse Derivan Gel Medium; Paper, Die-cuts & Rub-ons: Foof-a-La®

Use manila tags to form pages for the book. Cut chipboard pieces 1/2" bigger than the tags to form covers. Paint gel medium onto the chipboard and place face down onto the back side of the patterned paper. Flip patterned paper over and brayer to remove any bubbles. Take a piece of sandpaper and begin to lightly sand until you see lines forming where the edges of the chipboard lay. Sand firmly over these lines until you can gently tear the paper off from the edges of the chipboard. Embellish cover with rub-on and chipboard letter. Line up tags and covers and punch holes; bind with metal rings.

< WINTER 2006 *by* **EMILY**
supplies > Adhesive: Derivan Matisse Gel Medium; Jewel Frame: Advantus; Paint: Matisse Derivan; Paper & Chipboard Letters: Foof-a-La®

Cut the front and back covers off the spine of an old hardback book. (Now you have two pieces to work with for the new book.) Cover outside of the pieces in gel medium and cover with patterned paper. Firmly sand the edges of the book. Sand all four sides until you can gently pull away the excess paper. Paint the inside of the book covers with a layer of gesso. When dry, top with acrylic paint. Replace the covers back onto the spine with bookbinding tape. Cut and score several pieces of cardstock to form inner pages. Line up the scored line with the middle of the bookbinding tape and use an anywhere punch to punch two holes in spine. Thread and tie a strip of silk fabric through to hold the book together. Embellish cover with title and snowflake.

^ BOXED BIRDIES *by* **JENNIFER**

supplies > Chenille Stem: Westrim; Paper & Rub-ons: Foof-a-La®

Apply rub-on to one side of a small, clear, acrylic gift box to create a "window" to view the bird. Adhere patterned paper to inside and outside of box, covering all sides except for the top and "window" sides. Create a little nest for each bird using a section of cardboard toilet paper roll, chenille pipe cleaners and millinery flowers. Adhere bird to nest and the nest to the box with hot glue. Create finial for the top of the box using wooden craft embellishments and millinery flowers. Using a black felt pen, write label on white cardstock and trim into a banner shape and attach to finial. Hot glue finial and label to top of box.

< STAR BOOK *by* **JENNI**

supplies > Stamps: PSX; Stickers & Flower: Foof-a-La®

Cut a simple shape into an old book using a jigsaw. Find the approximate middle of book and flatten out or break the spine so it will sit open. Embellish opening with photos, stickers, buttons and charms. Display book on an easel.

^ Vintage Treasures by Becky
supplies > Paper, Flowers & Flourishes: Foof-a-La®; Stamps: Hero Arts

Remove chipboard lining from an old quilted sewing box and use as pattern to line the inside of box with paper. Before gluing down papers, stitch a loop of velvet ribbon onto the paper to be used on the inside of the lid. Glue down papers and add wool to the bottom of box. Stamp title onto label and mat with patterned paper and wool. Adhere to inside of lid. Embellish with canvas flowers, buttons, trim and millinery flowers.

< Crowning Glory by Becky
supplies > Paper, Die-cuts & Stickers: Foof-a-La®; Gems: Westrim; Pens: Sharpie, Zig

Create chipboard album by cutting four sheets of 5"x 7" chipboard and punch two holes to bind it. Set aside. Create each page as a mini layout and glue to the chipboard after assembling. Make the cover by layering patterned paper with book paper, tag, stitching and a rub-on. Add embellished crown die cut and letters along with pompom trim.

^ JACK THE JACK-O-LANTERN *by* **KIM**

supplies > Felt & Tag: Artist's Personal Stash; Buttons: Foof-a-La®

Felt is always fun to work with! You can cut it into any shape -- letters, shapes, swirls, frames and more. Felt can be adhered to paper or fabric with embroidery floss or glue. One of the best parts about using felt is the price -- it's very reasonable. There are several reasons why Kim loves each season, so she thought she would showcase each season by cutting out a shape to represent just that. Jack-O-Lanterns always make her smile!

< LOVE, HAPPILY EVER AFTER (STITCHING SAMPLER) *by* **KIM**

supplies > Muslin: P&B Textiles; Paper, Die-cut Tag, Stickers, Twill & Buttons: Foof-a-La®; Pens: Zig; Ribbon: May Arts, Raffit Ribbon & Mokuba

Hand stitching has been one of Kim's passions for many years. She loves incorporating it into her paper art projects to give them a homespun feel. You can find designs to stitch everywhere -- in coloring books, sewing patterns, children's drawings and more. Kim did this little primitive sampler on a road trip without a pattern; she just randomly stitched until she thought it looked complete. She used variegated embroidery floss for a very colorful look.

Tear light-colored cotton fabric to desired size. Use a permanent marking pen to draw stitching lines on fabric. Hand stitch over drawn lines. Cut batting and backing to the size of the quilt top and layer the pieces. Hand stitch embellishments (photo, buttons, felt squares, patterned paper, transparencies, twill and pipe cleaners) to quilt, binding the three layers together.

∧ Floral Cone *by* Teresa
supplies > Paper, Twill & Rub-ons: Foof-a-La®

Create a large cone shape from poster board and cover with patterned and vintage papers. Glue poster board into cone shape. Cut large border trim and glue to top of cone. Glue thin velvet ribbon to top of border. Punch a hole on left and right sides of cone and thread ribbon for hanging. Scallop punch a large circle and add monogram rub-on in center. Tie ribbons and twill to right side of hanger along with the scalloped monogram. Insert flowers into cone. Insert a welcome sign into a fork, then insert fork into center of flowers.

< Chairs in My Home *by* Marilyn
supplies > Beads: Westrim; Paper, Stickers & Rub-ons: Foof-a-La®; Varnish: Americana

Paint chairs with white acrylic paint. Paint other parts as desired. Let dry between coats. Finish with a protective coat of clear varnish. Allow to dry thoroughly. Scan and resize old cabinet card portraits. Print onto glossy paper; cut out. Embellish each bust and adhere to backs of chairs along with words. Wrap borders around chair seat. Fold paper into points and add to seats. Apply rub-ons and stickers and apply beads with glue.

^ **Us** by **Becky**
supplies > Paper, Buttons, Twill & Rub-ons: Foof-a-La®; Pen: Sakura; Photos: Tara Pakosta

Cover background of framed bulletin board with old book pages. Mat photos with patterned paper, using scalloped scissors on one side. Apply rub-ons to an oval of patterned paper matted on chipboard to create the title. Embellish board with ribbon, twill, buttons and handwritten labels.

> **Soldered Necklace** by **Teresa**
supplies > Letters, Paper, Buttons & Rub-ons: Foof-a-La®

Create a mini collage under two pieces of glass using snips of patterned papers and rub-on crown. Solder edges of glass and solder jump ring and chain. Glue rhinestones around soldered border on front of charm.